I
Hear
the
Birds
Sing

NARINE ASHNALIKYAN

I

Hear

the

Birds

Sing

For those who lost loved ones, for those who lost their health, for those who lost their friends, for those who lost their jobs, for those who lost themselves. For the brokenhearted, for you who feel weighed down with grief, in pain. For you whose days are so dark. For you barely hanging on.

I wrote this book for you.

There were many days I lay in bed, stricken with grief. My body hurt. My brain, my heart, and my soul felt numb. There was too much pain. I didn't know how I could get up. Then, one morning, I heard the birds sing. It was the sweetest sound I had ever heard.

Dear reader, may you find your breath again.
May you feel the sun's warmth on your skin.
I hope you hear the birds sing.

When people ask me why I decided to be a poet, I can't explain to them how I feel energy. How when I look into someone's eyes, I see heaviness. I see regret. I can't tell them that when I look at the sky, I see my ancestors shining. That I talk to my unborn children and tell them all the great things they will do when their souls choose their bodies. When people ask me why I decided to be a poet, I can't tell them that when I'm not speaking, I'm dying. And my body feels pain when I'm not writing. That for this empath, emotion is too strong to not be shared, that it rots when it stays within me. That when I speak, new life is birthed. That each poem is a gift to the sky. To each ancestor, and to each descendant. So I tell them, *I didn't choose to be a poet, the calling chose me.*

A bird doesn't sing because it has an answer, it sings because it has a song.

Maya Angelou

CONTENTS

Chapter 1. Armenian   *1*

Chapter 2. Effects of Trauma   *21*

Chapter 3. Heartbreak   *43*

Chapter 4. Love   *59*

Chapter 5. Healing   *83*

Chapter 6. Redemption   *97*

Chapter 7. Purpose   *113*

CHAPTER 1

Armenian

AFTER DINNER

Mom eats bread
with white cheese,
a slice of watermelon
and pomegranates.
Dad eats baklava
with black tea,
sunflower seeds
and dried apricots.
Grandmother eats
black olives, bread
with white cheese,
green grapes,
and little chocolates,
while Grandfather
sits quietly.
In the kitchen,
Sister washes the dishes,
and I stir thick,
Armenian coffee
in its little pot,
take a sip,
and taste
its bitterness
and strength.

BEAUTY

My mother removed
the black eye shadow
with a washcloth,
removed the foundation
that covered my skin,
removed the red lipstick
from my lips.
She held my face—
This, she said,
is beauty.

MY GRANDMOTHER IN AMERICA

At Grandma's house,
we eat *khingyali* and *pirashki*,
and she wants me to eat more
even when I'm full.

You bring me so much joy,
she says, *come over more often.*
She grew up in Syria,
and raised five daughters in Armenia.

She made her own cheese
and baked fresh bread.
She told her girls to clean the house,
to learn how to be good wives.

Today, when we sit around the dinner table,
Grandma sings in Arabic, in Armenian,
and sometimes when she sings,
she nods and cries.

Dark, strong, resilient, hopeful,
the will to rise above all—
what I see in Armenian eyes.

In my culture,

we don't talk about problems,

things that make us cry,

we don't talk about what happens

after we get married.

CONVERSATION WITH MOM AND GRANDMA

Topic: Men

Me: I don't understand them. It takes them so long to grow up.

Mom: Sometimes they never grow up.

Me: They're just so different, they're like animals.

Grandma: That's exactly what your grandfather was.

I wish my grandfather was a softer man, he was the only grandpa I had. I met him when I was 13. With excitement, I expected warm hugs and kind stories. But he was a handshake type of man. A harsh man. Tired from grueling decades of hard work and raising five children. I believe that he wanted to be kind, but didn't know how. It's been more than a year since he died, and I remember praying for him on his deathbed. I asked him if he wanted to accept Jesus as his savior. His body shook, his face lit up.

DAUGHTER OF IMMIGRANTS

When I think of what they did, I don't know if I could do it. They left their Motherland and arrived in a strange land. This place will never be home. The people don't look like them. The people don't sound like them. The food doesn't taste the same. Their children are so different from them. They take on characteristics from the strange land. *They* are a little foreign too.

Don't stay silent,
my ancestors warn me.
We brought you here
so you could be free.

WHEN THEY ASK ME
WHAT MY CULTURE IS KNOWN FOR

The wine and the apricots,
tragedy and celebration,
family and inherited family,
art, dancing, and loss.
Love, weddings, babies, and heartache.
There are the men—
strong, resilient, hardworking.
And then there are the women.
The Armenian woman is beauty,
she is hospitality,
she is the apricot and the wine,
she is art, she is love, she is the celebration.
The Armenian Woman is
the essence of our culture,
I tell them.

MY AUNT XHATUN

Armenia

Xhatun grew up in a little
house with chickens
and fresh eggs.

As a young girl,
she swam in rapid rivers
and was not afraid.

She married at seventeen
and left Mother Armenia,
to live with her husband in Russia.

Russia

The cold hurts
her bones
and cracks her skin.

The winter lasts
for ten months—
snow upon snow.

The trees shiver
skinny branches
no leaves in the crisp air.

Xhatun is a florist,
and says, *There is no color
here, except in the*

*imported flowers—
and the Russians,
they're as cold as the weather.*

America

In Los Angeles, Xhatun
walks in the sunshine
in sunglasses, shorts, and sandals—

she knows the name
and origin of each flower
in my garden.

She points to the sky,
and says, *Wow,*
what a beautiful blue.

She rests her head
on my mother's shoulder,
and sighs, *Sister.*

In my kitchen,
she dries the dishes
and dances.

She says, *Life is music,*
people should always
be dancing.

Black hair against white skin,
and long legs, she reminds me
of a piano key.

Xhatun walks onto my balcony,
and watches a hummingbird
drink from a flower.

Bare feet against
the warm ground,
she stands and sings.

for the grandfather I never met

HIS HANDS

My grandfather has beautiful hands.
They are scarred from the years
he spent fixing our neighbors' roofs.
He severed his finger carving my name
on a jewelry box.
He made me a polished dining room table,
and built my house.
I find my grandfather's thumbprints
on light bulbs and kitchen pipes.
His paintings are framed
on the walls of my home—
our family, Mount Ararat,
horses, and bottles of wine.
In the front yard,
he turns dirt with a shovel,
and together we plant tomatoes, lemons,
and yellow roses in my garden.

When I was a child,
I didn't like that my parents
made me speak Armenian.
But now, I'm thankful
because I haven't forgotten
my ancient native tongue—
I didn't know then, the power
of our beautiful, Հայերեն.

MY ARMENIA

I dream of you.
I dream of the day

I will hold your soil,
rub the grains,

and feel them spill
between my fingers.

I dream of the day
I will walk on your dirt,

your grass,
beneath my feet.

I touch the broken bricks
of your old churches

and feel the sharp edges scrape
against my skin.

I hear the children laugh
and I smile at how they sound like you.

I cup your bubbly water
with my hand

and bring it to my mouth
for a sweet taste.

My Armenia, I dream of you
and when I meet you, I will dance

to the beat of your drums,
eat the flesh of your fruit.

When I hear the beat of our drums
in Armenian music,
my whole body moves.
I kick my legs,
I raise my arms.
Every cell in my body fills with joy
and my life extends.
Perhaps it was this—
the memories, the drums,
our music that saved us.

-

We are spread out over the Earth, but our language binds us. Our love is endless, we would die for each other. They try to kill us, but we rise up together. Around the dinner table, we eat dolmas, apricots, and pomegranates. We drink bitter coffee, black tea, red wine. We dance to the drums. We sing, we laugh. We cry with the duduk, we share stories and remember. Armenian, when I meet you, I know the blood in your veins runs in my veins. I shake your hand, we say, Բարեւ, and I see the strength in your eyes, the resilience in your spirit.

CHAPTER 2

Effects of Trauma

For the longest time,
I didn't write.

They told me I was stupid
and I believed them.

DREAMS

1. She is chronically ill. Her arms are bent the wrong way. She walks with a limp. She got sicker and sicker every year. *Why are you so sick,* I asked. *Because I didn't follow my dreams,* she replied, *I was too afraid.*

2. This morning, I woke up in pain. My shoulders, my legs, and my arms carried burdens.

3. Every cell in my body begged me, *Narine, write the book.*

I can't drink away these sorrows.
Pain flows in my blood—
this body felt loss
from the moment it was born.

GENOCIDE

1.

The sand grazes my great grandmother's
eyes as she crosses the Syrian Desert.

She cries. The moans of her
dying friends echo in her ears.

The sun burns her flesh.
The smell of dead bodies linger.

2.

When I was young, a dark figure
followed me in my dreams.

Sometimes, I feel death
when I lie down to sleep.

One night I woke up and screamed—
I knew I was alive.

What hurts the most?
I ask her.
Loss, she replies.

-conversations with my body

Doctors say that women carry trauma that pass down to their grandchildren. That the lives they had affect the genes of their offspring's offspring. My grandmother told me about the man who had taken her to a river, put a gun to her head, and forced her to marry. *I'm a child,* she said, *I don't want to get married.* But she wanted to live. She cried and wrote a letter to her family convincing them she wanted this marriage. In my dreams, a man runs after me with a gun. *No!* I yell. *No, you can't get me!*

In my dream, you died and your ghost watched me sleep. *What do you want,* I asked. *I just wanted to stop by,* you said. Sometimes it's not you, black shadows follow me. But I know it's you. When I get dressed in the morning, I pick the shoes that would be the easiest to run in. I walk to the coffee shop and I'm thinking about the three huddled guys in the corner outside of the parking lot. A guy walks into a cafe with a cap on, his hood over his cap, and a black mask. I listen to the performer and I keep looking back at him. I tell myself, *if he takes a gun out, lie on the ground. Lie on the ground and play dead.*

As a child, I would go to a lake with my family,
and we'd walk across white bridges.
I enjoyed the dark green hills,
the smell of the trees,
the ducks in the pond.
But when I saw the peacocks,
I grew jealous—
I wished I was that free.

When I'm around you,
I feel like I'm drowning.
I keep trying to come up for air,
but your energy is a hand on my face
pushing pushing pushing me down underwater.

I used to let you walk all over me
because I thought that's what women
were supposed to do.

My back hurt
from hunching over—
from making myself
so small.

Every cell in my body tells me to leave you.

My body is tired,
it's detoxing from
the jealous one
the liar
the creep
the flake—
you.

My mind forgot the trauma,
but my body didn't.

Everything made sense,
when you whispered,
Sometimes I hate myself.

I wish I knew who you were before all the pain changed you.
I wonder if we would've been closer.
In my dream, I gave birth to you so you could start over,
so you could be free.

For years, I stayed silent.
I didn't even recognize
the sound of my own voice.

Some days, I can't feel my fingers. I can't feel the breath that escapes me. Some days, I can't feel the wind touch my face. I can't feel my heart beat, and I wonder if I'm still alive.

Like Job,
I lost everything
my friends
my money
my health.
Each day I suffered
felt like an eternity.
I looked up—
take this away from me
or take me.

CHAPTER 3

Heartbreak

I didn't know I needed you
until I almost had you.

I moved mountains
for you,
but you walked
around them.

NOTES ON MIRRORS

You tell me to be quiet—
everyone is staring.
You don't wait for me,
and walk ahead of me.
You never stroke my hair,
or dance so close
you can smell my skin—so sweet.
You never write me songs,
or sing to me, or hold my feet
and measure the curves with your fingers.
You don't kiss my bare shoulder,
or rest your head on my chest
and listen to me breathe.
You never hold my face in your hands
and tell me that you love the way I laugh.
You don't whisper in my ear,
or leave little notes on mirrors,
or green grapes or chocolate truffles
on my coffee table.
You don't speak my language.

In my back pocket
a crumpled piece
of paper—
the love letter
you gave me.

I didn't know I was addicted to you
until I went through withdrawals.

When you said you didn't deserve me,
I should've believed you.

I feel sadness in my bones—
my arms feel heavy,
feel empty
without you.

I've been broken many times.
Why does this time feel
like a special sort of brokenness?
Like you meant to do it all along.

I go to the river
and wash my hands.
I take a sip,
swim in its waters,
but the very thought of you
still makes me feel dirty.

My poems have
more love in them
than you ever
gave me.

Several years of tests—
you too were a test.

If I could be born again,
I would come back as your father,
and teach you what it takes
to earn the love
of a good woman.

I had a dream you came back,
held my face,
and said, *It's you,*
it was always you.
But, I replied,
it was never you.

When I held your hand,
I felt like nothing could break me.

But when you left,
you took the very last breath of me.

Everything changed—
even the sky looked gray.

But today, I heard
two birds sing to each other.

Their songs woke me up.
I looked out my window

and saw them fly off
into the bright blue sky.

CHAPTER 4

Love

I see you every time
I close my eyes—
tall and unafraid.

In my dream, a red hummingbird told me,
Your love is coming.
I sit at a park
and stare at a beautiful flower.
Two red hummingbirds
drink from that flower,
look at my face
and fly away.

I can't sleep—
I'm suddenly aware
of the empty space around me.
It's too quiet,
I'm aware of the darkness.

Sometimes I imagine myself alone
and I feel peace, I feel at home.
But you show up in my dreams,
you tell me to wait,
you tell me you're coming.
In the mornings,
I walk into my kitchen,
take out two cups
and brew coffee.

I feel the diminishing of everything that was in between you and me.

When I close my eyes,
I see your face—
strong lines and soft eyes.

Every time I feel your energy,
a butterfly flies right in front of me,
reminds me to look up and look ahead,
tells me you're coming.

When I found you, I knew,
I finally came back home.

YOU WROTE ME A POEM

You lit lavender candles
and put a vase of purple orchids
on my coffee table.
You made stuffed grape leaves,
washed my dishes,
and gave me little chocolates.
You taught me the tango.
You learned my language.

I'd rather see the ugly you.

The part you think no one wants to see.

The part you try to hide.

I want to see the you that rises up.

I want to know what makes you mad.

I prefer tenderness.

Tell me, what did your last love do? You keep me at an arm's length.
I see the fear in your eyes. I see you coming closer, then running away.
Tell me, what broke you so bad that the pieces are still crushing you?

I'll love you so well, you'll forget you were ever broken.

If I could, I would tattoo
your scent on my body.

When I look at you, I see the sunrise
and the sunset at the same time.
I see the ocean,
I feel the wind in my hair,
I hear the birds sing.

BLUE JAYS SANG IN MY DREAM

The tips of my fingers reached,
but couldn't wipe the dust
off the surface of the moon.

I raised my hands to feel the current of the wind,
and a stranger caught them,
took my right hand, and spun me.

I couldn't stop turning,
and fell into a pile of leaves
left over from autumn.

I tiptoed across the ocean
so the moon wouldn't hear me,
but I knew it was listening.

The waves brought me back to shore,
and I walked across the grains of sand,
and danced to the singing of the jays.

Blue birds mating on a branch,
big butterflies,
bumblebees, birch trees,
books of poetry—
every beautiful thing reminds me of you.

As the sun rises to wake the Earth,
I think of you,
how your light illuminates my life
and your smile carries my burdens.
And when I hold your hand,
the troubles in my heart dissipate
as if they never belonged to me.

When I'm not with you,
I look for you.
The sound of your laugh
follows me in my dreams.
Throughout the day,
I wonder what you're doing
and who you're talking to.
I feel crazy,
I'm so consumed by you.
No one has captured me
the way you do—
when you hold my hand,
I feel as though you're holding my heart.
When you look in my eyes,
we tell each other stories
of how we met lifetimes ago
and we see our whole future.

Your love teaches me how to be soft.

We sit in silence and laugh out loud.
You start talking and I finish your sentence.
I cook your favorite food,
you bake my favorite dessert.
I run over to tell you something,
I know, you say.
I can tell from the look
on your face.

No amount of romantic books,
love songs,
even Neruda's poetry
compares to our love.
How we were lovers
and dancers in a past life,
royalty in another,
how every time we die and are reborn,
our souls wander back to each other
because we still
haven't had enough.

CHAPTER 5

Healing

Sometimes it's my imagination that saves me.

After being told to be quiet for so long,
I thought my voice didn't matter.
Now, I have learned how to speak.
I won't apologize for saying no,
for saying I want more meat
and less vegetables.
I want the onions grilled.
I only like sweet wine,
how sweet is this?

There was so much clutter in my mind,

it spilled over into my room,

into my car, into my kitchen.

I couldn't find the black pepper,

so I bought more.

Solitude gave me time to rest,

to put everything back in order,

and release you.

You remind me of a drug
I was once addicted to—
it made me crazy,
it made me weak.
No thanks,
I tell you,
I'm sober now.

Everything was better after you left.

I shed layers off my skin,
off my back,
these burdens are too heavy to carry—
insecurity, doubt, fear,
you're not a part of my DNA,
you haven't touched
the new skin I live in.

I used to be so hard,
I never cried.
Now I'm so soft,
I look at a bird and cry,
Look how it flies so free.

I wasn't born kind,
I carry troubles in my heart.
They make me better,
they make me kind.

I used to hate the ends of things.
I closed my fists so nothing would be
taken away from me.
Loyal to a fault,
I held on for too long.
Now, I leave my hands open—
everything belongs to the sun.
In a moment, a bird flies and rests on my hand,
and in the next, it flies away.

I used to think about the future
and see darkness.
I never thought this state would exist.
Peace. Confidence. Hope.

I hold my feet and send love
to my whole body.
I hold my 5-year-old self
and tell her she's stronger
than she'll ever know.
My hands let go of you,
let go of us,
they hold precious things now—
they hold my feet now.

The skin on my hands
keep peeling,
keep shedding
the memories of you.
These new hands,
have never held yours.

CHAPTER 6

Redemption

I heard your name over and over.
You followed me everywhere I went,
you followed me in my dreams.
I knew your story,
but I knew *You*
when you resurrected me.

ENCOUNTERS WITH GOD

When I was five, I'd look outside my bedroom window
and wonder what would happen if I fell.

In my dream, I looked outside that window and saw Jesus.
I knew one day, I would follow Him.

Before I got baptized, a priest put oil on my forehead.
I saw God smiling at me, I couldn't speak.

I was seven when I read the gospel for the first time.
I tried to make myself forget it, but I couldn't.

You have life because Jesus gave you life.

-answers from dreams

I came to love the very things
I judged when I was younger.

I look for love in each of their faces,
they come and go, come and go.
My heart tries to fill the void
with their attention—
I look in the mirror,
You are enough,
I tell her.

I get scared to have children when I think about all the times I've been touched as a child without permission. I think about each person. Their name. Their brokenness. And how the world isn't a safe place for children. There is so much darkness in the world. How can I bear to see my kids hurt or suffer the pain I've suffered? But the darker they are out there, the better I become. The further I want to be from their darkness. I walk into the light. My compassion grows. I will be kinder. I will love stronger. I will be a safe place for my children and all children.

1. Little by little,
    I let them tell me
    who I was—
    I lost myself.

2. Everything they built in me,
    I tore down,
    burned it to ashes
    and built myself back
    with fire and compassion.

I used to look in the mirror
and hate looking at my sad eyes.
Those eyes judged me,
told me I wasn't enough.
I allowed other people's voices
to tell me I wouldn't make it.
I was so fearful,
there were days I didn't move.
I stood in silence.
Now, I look in the mirror
and strong eyes
look back at me.
You can do anything, I tell her,
everything you need is already inside you.

I used to think negatively of weakness. I'd put a smile on to show my strength. I would never cry. I built walls around me that no one could climb over. I learned that in my vulnerability, the walls crumbled. The space between you and me became smaller. In my weakness, you held my hand.

When I look at the sun
or the moon,
and listen to the birds
in the air,
I can't help but think of you—
how you light up the dark
and the day,
how even the smell of you
makes flowers bloom.

Before I went to sleep,
I prayed, *God show me*
what I need to do,
I can't take this anymore.
That night, I had a dream
I was in a classroom.
I took a black marker
and started drawing
on a whiteboard.
I drew a small dot
and a large wave that
stretched across three boards.
The amount of hopelessness,
I have experienced is a speck
compared to the amount of hope
I found when I knew God, I told them.
The hope you have in God
will not disappoint you.
It is that hope that saves me.

Science says matter and energy are neither created nor destroyed.

They are transformed from one form to another.

When you died, you found a new home in her womb.

I hold her baby, wide eyed and curious.

I look in his eyes and he smiles at me.

And I remember your last words,

I'll see you soon.

I feel everything getting away from me
and coming to me at the same time.
As if my old life is being swept up
in a tornado and split to dust into the sky.
As if my new life is emerging like the rising sun—
bright, beautiful, glorious.

Under the still moon,
whcn I pray,
I hear God breathe.

CHAPTER 7

Purpose

What is my purpose?
I asked the bird.
It looked straight to the sky
and flew to the sun.

The sun doesn't ask the sky if it belongs.

David needed a Goliath to triumph
and get to the next level.
You were my Goliath.

I know who I am and where I'm going.
You can't stop me.
Go ahead, try and tell me that I can't do it.
That it's too late or I'll never make it.
You'll see my face,
you'll hear my name
everywhere you go.

Don't teach your girls how to be polite
otherwise they may never learn how to say,
No.
I don't like that.
I don't give you permission.
NO.
Don't teach your girls how to be polite,
otherwise they will spend their whole lives
trying to please everyone else
and be stuck
as someone's daughter, wife, mother
with no idea of who they are.
Don't teach your girls how to be polite
teach them how to speak.
How to speak their dreams into existence.
How to say I already am
a writer
a speaker
a singer
a dancer
a doctor
a CEO.
I am that.
I don't have to marry that.
Don't teach your girls how to be polite,
teach them that women are strong.
That they can be,
that they are
everything.

I won't let my feet
walk away from me.
I return to myself
over and over again.

I talk to my soul,
remind her that she is loved
that she is a treasure,
that she was born because
the universe needed her —
craved her very existence.

Sometimes you have to sit on the train
and allow God's grace to take you
to your next destination.

-advice from my pastor

The darkness follows me,
You can't do it
I'm watching you,
I'm here,
it tells me.
I walk forward
and it shatters from my light.

Tests come to distract me,
they grow like the weeds in my garden.
Tirelessly, I remove them again and again.
I press on with the end goal in mind—
my voice will move the world.

This whole time
I thought I was looking for you,
but I was looking for myself.
This year,
I found her.
I haven't put my pen down,
my new voice emerges,
it's louder now.
Mic in hand,
I wear my crown
and walk onto my stage.

In my youth,
I may have chosen
the bitter one
the aggressive one
the selfish one,
the one my gut said
is my next mistake.
But in wisdom,
I choose myself.

You can come and go,
I've met many of you,
and if you do decide to leave,
I still have myself.

I never thought the best and worst year of my life would be the same year. The year I felt utter grief. Sad days upon sad days with no end in sight. But it was in that year I was awakened—what was dead, came to life. I left who I didn't want to be and became who I am.

I talk to my unborn children,
You're going to be world changers,
I tell them,
you're going to be just like your mom.

.